This journal
belongs to

....

....

100
Days
to
Calm

A Journal for
Finding Everyday Tranquility

Amy Leigh Mercree

STERLING ETHOS
New York

STERLING ETHOS
New York

An Imprint of Sterling Publishing Co., Inc.
1166 Avenue of the Americas
New York, NY 10036

ISBN 978-1-4549-4029-6

Distributed in Canada by Sterling Publishing Co., Inc.
c/o Canadian Manda Group, 664 Annette Street
Toronto, Ontario M6S 2C8, Canada
Distributed in the United Kingdom by GMC Distribution Services
Castle Place, 166 High Street, Lewes, East Sussex BN7 1XU, England
Distributed in Australia by NewSouth Books
University of New South Wales, Sydney, NSW 2052, Australia

For information about custom editions, special sales, and premium
and corporate purchases, please contact Sterling Special Sales at
800-805-5489 or specialsales@sterlingpublishing.com.

Manufactured in Singapore

2 4 6 8 10 9 7 5 3 1

sterlingpublishing.com

Cover design by Elizabeth Mihaltse Lindy
Interior design by Shannon Nicole Plunkett

Cover and interior illustrations by Nikiparonak/Shutterstock.com

• • •

This book is dedicated
to my radiant medicine teacher,
Laurie "Levity Laughing Star" Farrell.
Now she is singing among the stars,
weaving light and healing for all.

• • •

Introduction

Welcome to your 100 days to calm. If you picked up this journal because you are ready to relax and release your stress in an easy and fun way, you are in the right place.

Life in the twenty-first century is demanding, and anything that challenges your mind or body can create stress, positive or negative. Good stress is when you move through a tough work-out; bad stress is your boss demanding that report yesterday. Work difficulties, such as long hours or lack of compensation and appreciation, account for most stress, closely followed by relationships, including ones with family, and financial concerns. Perhaps the stealthiest form of stress is the free-floating fear and uncertainty that enters our lives through media. You've got to know when to switch that device off!

As a holistic health expert for over fifteen years, one of the main causes of disease and health ailments I see is stress. Stress is harder on your body than intense physical labor; it will break you down. Here are just a few of its most damaging effects: insomnia; depression, anxiety and panic attacks; colds, viruses, and infections from a weakened immune system; and circulatory problems due to veins that constrict due to stress. If you reduce stress, you'll be much healthier.

I have created a fun way for you to infuse your life with more tranquility. In this book you will enact small yet powerful changes to transform worry to serenity. My hope is that this journal helps you cultivate a daily ritual, a few minutes for just *you* to care for *yourself*, one that will help restore a sense of peace and calm throughout your day. Just the act of pausing long enough to write down your thoughts, feelings, and intentions will help you slow down and become more mindful of what is happening around you and, more importantly, inside of you. Conscious mindful actions that are practiced consistently can make a big difference.

I am here to reconnect you to you and provide the tools you need for a calmer, healthier, happier life. I'll teach you simple meditation, and I include visualization exercises that will allow you to conjure peaceful images to ease your stress and help you breathe more deeply. You will find prompts for collecting your thoughts on calm and writing down your ideas and feelings. You'll also find mindfulness-related activities that will sharpen your ability to see the world around you as it is; you will hone your intuition, and your decisions will become easier.

I want you to feel serene and relaxed and to experience joy and pleasure in your life. With this journal, let's journey together into benevolence, ease, and happiness and discover the beauty of calm.

XO,

Amy Leigh Mercree

How to Use This Journal

This journal was created with ultimate ease in mind. All you need to complete most of these entries is a pen or pencil. You can work through the activities sequentially, whether you're ready to commit to 10 or 100 sequential days of calm, but it's not a prerequisite for enjoying this journal. Your conscious mindful actions might be sporadic, and sometimes you may need extra support to come back to your own sense of serenity. Or you might be ready to jump in and commit to a specific amount of time. No matter what your situation, this journal will be your cozy companion in both times of stress and in times of peace.

If you prefer to skip around, feel free to choose the activity that suits you and your mood in the moment. You can flip through the pages before deciding, or you can open to a page at random, trusting that that the activity you find is the one that you need at that moment.

Most of the activities in this journal are meant to be completed within 5 to 10 minutes. You can use this journal at any time of day or night. If you have a hard time falling asleep, perhaps complete a prompt every night before bed. If you face challenging days, do it every morning when you wake up.

Finding a quiet spot at lunchtime is great way to slow your heartbeat and find your center during a stressful work day. You can also slip off and find a quiet corner of your home. Practice finding your calm in a carpool line, on a train, plane, or bus, or even as you stroll down the street. In times of great stress, you may need to use some tools in one moment and others in the next. Remember, there are no rules with this journal. When you need to relax, it will always be here for you.

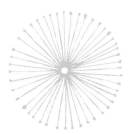

Day 1

Meditation can be a powerful tool for inducing a sense of calm, especially if practiced regularly. There are a myriad of health benefits to regular meditation. Not only does it improve your focus and ability to concentrate, it also helps balance your mood and improves the functions of your physical body, including your nervous system.

Your nervous system often plays a big role when you experience feelings of worry or anxiety. It becomes overstimulated and, well, nervous, responding to hormones from your adrenal glands, your brain, and other parts of your body. When the nervous system is overstimulated, you feel on edge.

Meditation is one of the most powerful tools for turning anxiousness into tranquility. Even a few minutes of practice two to three times per week can make a significant difference. The more meditation you fit into your day, the calmer, clearer, and more creative you will feel.

Today, you can get started with a simple meditation. Sit quietly and repeat the word *peace* in your mind. Every time a thought arises, simply repeat the word peace. Begin with a goal of meditating for 5 minutes. You'll find your mind wandering a great deal at the beginning (the practice of yoga refers to these wandering thoughts as "mind weeds"). As you become more comfortable, increase your time to 10 minutes and continue to build for as long as your day allows you.

Did this simple meditation help you feel calmer? Was it challenging to remember to bring your thoughts back to the word *peace*?

_____

_____

_____

_____

_____

_____

_____

_____

_____

_____

_____

_____

_____

_____

_____

_____

_____

Day 2

Mindfulness is an important concept in Buddhist philosophy. All it requires is that you be in the moment, alert to all that is happening around you. You do not need to judge anything as good or bad. Lately, mindfulness it has become trendy—and for good reason. It's powerful stuff. The ancient practice is used widely today to cease harmful rumination and self-criticism, a huge component of stress. When you let go of the past and cease being the inner critic, you've opened yourself to calm.

Being mindful can be elusive for many of us living modern lifestyles. It's impossible to be present to a singular moment when we're multitasking and constantly checking our phones for emails, texts, likes, follows, DMs, or notifications. How in the world can we clear it all away and experience mindfulness?

Yesterday is the memory. Tomorrow is a fantasy. Mindfulness is now. If we can separate ourselves from the noise of the world and allow ourselves to be fully present in the moment, we can feel the pleasure and ecstasy that life brings us more deeply and experience happiness in a deep, rich way.

- We all spend time washing dishes, so let's use that as our first example of mindfulness. In this moment, choose complete focus on your hands, the soap, the water, and the dirty dish. Notice your surroundings. What is your body touching? How you feel? What is the sensation of water flowing over your hands? Does the soap pile up? Play with the suds, and stack your dishes. What do you sense and feel now?

Day 3

Contemplate the following phrase: "You have everything you need." What does that mean, exactly? It means you have limitless potential to learn, change, grow, run, jump, and be still. No matter the stress you feel today, you can handle it. You are perfect and perfectly capable of learning how to navigate life with a feeling of clarity and calm. If you begin to think of any limitations, remember that they are an illusion. The truth is you are unlimited.

In this meditation activity, you will tap into this truth and feel it on a visceral level. Close your eyes and contemplate the present moment and its unlimited potential. Inhale deeply, and exhale slowly as you let this idea sink in. Sit with this for a few moments. Notice how you feel. Know that no matter what rushes toward you, you have what you need: you have you.

As you meditate and learn more about yourself, you'll feel a new strength. That strength might build trust inside yourself or help you deal with what the world presents.

Describe how this felt in your body. Where did you notice it? Did your breathing slow?

Day 4

In our joyful quest for calm, we'll tap into the power of movement. Sometimes moving our bodies can bring the ultimate sense of contentment, and as you continue with your day, you may notice that you feel much more serene and energized. Choose a song that you absolutely love and that brings you a sense of peace. You might consider choosing a song that doesn't have a lot of lyrics.

Press Play, and put your song on repeat. As your song plays, allow yourself to move. You can begin by standing, sitting, or lying down. Perhaps you're swaying or stepping from side to side. Let the sounds of the music penetrate the cells of your body. Pay attention to which movements feel best.

When you feel ready for stillness, press Stop, lie down on your back, and simply breathe. Notice how you feel. Observe any continuing movements and sensations inside your body. These sensations may tell you where your stress hides and what you need to work out. If you're breathing heavily, take deep cleansing breaths. Enjoy the silence, and observe the internal movement that continues inside your body. Allow your breath and heartbeat to return to a soft resting pattern.

- What song did you choose? In what ways did you feel the music through your body? What part of your body feels best after this exercise?

Day 5

Today, think about the interconnected nature of the universe. The same matter and energy that was generated by the explosion of a distant star was transported all the way across the galaxy to be the building blocks for our sun. The energy from the sun feeds the plants that make up the salad that you just ate for lunch.

Recognizing that we are nourished by the universe is one of many doorways to tranquility. Knowing that you're connected to everything gives you an opportunity to relax. You feel you are part of something larger than just you, and this brings you comfort and perspective. You can relax into the peace that is available to you. You can choose to rest in the present moment knowing that it is the only true reality.

How do you feel connected to the world around you?

Day 6

Bring your attention to the bottoms of your feet. Notice what they are touching, if anything. Do they feel the touch of the fabric of your socks? Are they being lightly caressed by your bedsheets? Are they exposed to the cool air? Are they pulsing or tingling in any way?

For this calming practice, we'll focus on the bottoms of our feet, the spot where we meet ground and stand tall. It's best to do this on real earth—grass or dirt please. Standing on natural ground in your bare feet has a name: "earthing." Many believe the electromagnetic energy of the Earth can return your blood pressure to normal and calms inflammation, among other things. While not scientifically proven, we do know that walking barefoot stimulates the bottoms of the feet, which can promote feelings of connectedness and improves balance.

Stand and feel how the bottoms of your feet connect with the ground beneath you. Feel the energy coming up through the souls of your feet. This is the place between Earth and sky that you inhabit. This is where your presence begins on this Earth. This is the place from which the feeling of being grounded and present in your physical body begins. Take a few minutes to allow yourself to feel this, both physically and mentally. Inhale and exhale deeply, allowing your breath to travel all the way into the bottoms of your feet.

- Write about how this experience of being grounded feels.

Day 7

Our emotions sometimes feel like they are too big to fit in one body, but being consciously aware of them can be one of the most healing choices you can make. We have long known that just naming a thing gives you power over it. When you are aware of how you feel, as opposed to repressing it, then your emotional energy keeps flowing and doesn't get stuck. You become less attached to your emotions because they flow like a river, unimpeded.

With this meditation, take a moment to take stock of how you feel. Place your hands on the center of your chest. Simply notice what emotions come up. You may feel empty. You may feel bursting with passion or simply a sense of contentment. You may feel heartbreak or sadness. Rest for a few minutes with your hands on your heart and be present to how you feel.

What emotions came up for you during this meditation? Did any of the feelings surprise you?

Day 8

Breathing supplies your body with the oxygen it needs to produce energy. Under stress, your breathing becomes rapid and shallow, depriving your body of what it most needs at the moment it needs it. Under stress, most people hold their breath or breathe in short shallow intakes. The heart rate quickens and needs more energy that it can't get because the oxygen isn't coming.

When you become more aware of how you breathe, you'll be able to keep your breathing deep and your heart rate even the next time you confront stress. You'll feel like a superhero passing through a meteor storm!

Try building awareness with this exercise. Begin to notice the breath moving in and out of your body. Breathe in through your nose, and bring the breath down into the base of your abdomen, filling your lungs from bottom to top. After you've inhaled as much as you possibly can, purse your lips and imagine that you have a straw in your mouth. Blow the air out as slowly and for as long as possible through this imaginary straw.

Repeat this breathing cycle two more times. After your last repetition, observe how you feel. For example, your body may feel more relaxed. Perhaps you've discovered that your lung capacity was a lot greater than you realized. Be present to any sensations, feelings, images, and thoughts that come up.

- How did you feel after completing this exercise? What did you notice?

Day 9

Let's practice another meditation, this one connecting you with everything that is: the universe. Carl Sagan once famously said, "We are made of star-stuff." What is up there in space, the materials that make up spinning planets and twinkling stars, is also inside you.

Find a comfortable seat or place to lie down. As you become comfortable, let your mind relax and your breath grow slow and deep. Imagine a giant sun or moon hovering over an ocean of black water. Your moon or sun can rise and fall in your imagination; track it with your mind's eye. Continue to breathe in and exhale deeply as you repeat the mantra *Earth, Sun, Moon, Infinity*. Feel the infinite space around your sun or moon as it rises and falls over the sea. Feel yourself as a part of what is and what will always be.

- What adjectives would you use to describe how that meditation felt?

- What did you imagine, a sun or moon? Describe what you saw and how you felt watching it rise and fall.

Day 10

Visualization is a powerful tool in the toolbox of calm. It is nothing more than imagining a picture in your mind. This can be done in less than a second anywhere. You can do it during a tense meeting at work, sitting in traffic, or during difficult moments with your kids. When you picture something you associate with peace and contentment, your breathing relaxes and oxygen moves in your body uninterrupted. Visualization can stabilize your mood when you feel it turning downward.

Here is an easy visualization exercise. Imagine yourself strolling in a garden. What does this garden look like? Is it full of flowers? Does it contain some of your favorite trees? Is it a wild, untamed garden, or is it a manicured, beautiful garden with stepping-stones and topiaries? What color are the flowers? What season is it?

As you notice this beautiful garden, allow yourself to sink into a sense of calm. Discover that there is a comfortable couch, chair, or a chaise longue upon which you could rest. Perhaps it's next to a gentle stream or a serene pond or lake. Let yourself lie or sit there and feel the beautiful energy of the garden around you. Allow yourself to open your being to the energy of the plant spirits there. What do they feel like? All around you there is life pulsing, teaming, enlivening you. What does that feel like? Let yourself rest in this visualization of the garden.

- Describe your garden in detail. What is this idyllic place like, and how did you feel when you were there?

Day 11

Today, I want you to look at your to-do list. If you don't have one handy, just write down what you would like to accomplish. Now, let's look at the list and break down the way you feel about it.

First, make notes about how the entire list impacts you. Does it affect your inner sense of serenity? With every line of your to-do list, ask yourself the same question. Are there patterns in your emotions? Are there repetitive elements on your to-do list that consistently cause you to be agitated, annoyed, or exhausted?

Next, think about whether you can adjust your point of view about each task. Perhaps that carpool line becomes less disagreeable if you attach it to the overall happiness and safety of your child. Painting the house is a week's worth of dedicated work, but the value it adds to your appreciation of beauty and the enjoyment of seeing a color you love daily is worth the effort. Learn to examine your to-do list with a fresh point of view.

Describe the initial emotions that each task on your to-do list evokes. Go line by line. Then, imagine a different way to perceive your tasks. Does this shift in perspective calm you?

Day 12

Meditation can provide a sense of serenity that comes from being present in the moment. In this meditation, we will use a mantra, a repeated word or sound that helps increase focus. A mantra helps keep your mind focused on something simple instead of the running commentary in your brain. The repetitive nature of a mantra allows you to enter into a deep state of relaxation.

You can use any two words for your mantra—it's up to you. If you want to rely on the mantra used by millions of practitioners, try *Om Shanti*. In Sanskrit, this mantra means "infinite peace." *Om* symbolizes the sound of creation. *Shanti* simply means "peace."

Get comfortable, and enjoy some deep breaths. Inhale deeply and then exhale slowly. As you breathe, repeat your mantra. Continue breathing and repeating your mantra for as long as you choose. Notice how wonderful that feels. If your mind wanders, that's okay. Just bring it back to the words you are repeating and clear your mind again. Do not try to force or push your mind to stay focused. Allow your thoughts to unravel themselves, and gently bring your attention back to your mantra each time you notice that your mind has wandered.

- Describe the sensations you experienced during this meditation. How did your body react when you repeated the mantra? Did you feel any specific emotions?

Day 13

The word *surrender* both frightens and delights. It suggests defeat for some. But I believe that surrender means opening yourself up to endless possibilities: peace, joy, and infinite potential. It means letting go of the past, of judgments, and of negative feelings that create stress and unhappiness and hold you back. Surrender, for me, is a freeing dive back into the joyous river of life. When you become receptive to surrender, you can find deeper rest and calm. You let go of struggle and release your tight hold, making room for your mind, body, and heart to expand.

Find a comfortable seat or place to lie down. Breathe deeply to repeat the mantra, "I surrender." Let those difficult thoughts and unpleasant memories go. Allow your heart to relax. Allow your consciousness to open and clear. Feel your shoulders and upper back melt as the muscles, nerves, tendons, and fascia unfurl.

- What did you notice when you opened to this idea of surrender? How did it feel?

- Did you let go of past judgments? Did old disharmonious feelings melt away? Completely, or a little bit?

Day 14

Sometimes keeping quiet can cause stress that leads us away from inner peace. Have you ever experienced someone talking over you? We fume, perhaps complaining behind his or her back. Horrible customer service leaves you enraged, but you bite your tongue because you have waited two months for that delivery.

What would happen if you could have calmly stated your objections and walked away?

It's time for you to speak up and own your unique voice. What you have to say is important. It's wise. And someone needs to hear it. Swallowing reactions, words, and feelings is not healthy. You may have doubted yourself in the past. You may have allowed fear or apprehension to paralyze you. You may have felt anxious to share your truth. The time to speak up is now. Share your feelings and needs unapologetically. Be your real self, and walk, talk, and live your truth while always keeping kindness in your heart. Only when we feel heard do we feel peace.

- In what situations do you avoid speaking up?

- Was there a situation today where you felt you could have said more? What did you need to say?

- Is there anything that you feel is stunting your self-expression or ability to advocate for yourself?

Day 15

In the quest for calm, you will discover that minimizing stress hormones, such as cortisol and adrenaline, will play a key role. All human beings have a lizard brain; it is a primitive mechanism where the "fight or flight" instinct lives. In a world of saber-toothed tigers or tyrannosaurus rexes, humans had to decide, in a blink of an eye, if they would flee or fight. The same happens to you now, even though evolution added many layers to your brain. The lizard area still activates when you feel under threat and floods your body with cortisol and adrenaline. Those two stress hormones, over time, can create anxiety, depression, and illness.

Meditation helps you avoid a fight-or-flight response every time you are faced with a stressful situation or thought, but there are other ways that we can minimize your stress hormones.

– Schedule vigorous exercise earlier in the day and gentle exercise later in the day.

– Try relaxation techniques like meditation, spend time in nature, and avoid digital screens for at least 30 minutes before bed.

– Avoid caffeine, sugar, and alcohol, especially during the six hours before bed.

– Take magnesium before bed—it calms the parasympathetic nervous system.

– Eat one serving of a low-glycemic healthy carbohydrate with dinner (like sweet potato or garbanzo beans) to help stabilize mood.

– Increase your consumption of organic fruits and vegetables, nuts, and seeds as well.

– Add tulsi tea to your nighttime routine. Tulsi tea, a derivative of the holy basil plant, has loads of magnesium, lowers cortisol levels, and assists blood vessels in opening and closing.

The foods you eat, the supplements you take, and the ways you spend your time have a direct impact on your health and how calm you feel from day to day. Sleep at least eight hours per night.

Try one of these strategies today. How did you respond? What did you notice?

_____

_____

_____

_____

_____

_____

_____

_____

_____

_____

_____

Day 16

The calming effects of water have been known for as long as humans can remember. Sixty percent of your body is made of water. Staying hydrated can flush toxins from the body and provide the building blocks for the blood and lymphatic fluid that moves nutrients and oxygen through the body, sustaining your energy levels. What does water do to the soul? Watching the ocean is both meditative and exciting; it is a reflection of both life's turbulence and quiet beauty. Water passing over skin calms and restores; you are truly in your element.

Hydrotherapy can be used to soothe distressed or weary bodies and minds. You may have practiced hydrotherapy at the gym in a sauna, steam room, or heated whirlpool. Today, you'll practice hydrotherapy closer to home, in the comfort of your own bathroom.

Fill your tub with water as hot as you can comfortably stand. You can also do this in the shower instead of running a bath. After your temperature is set, get in and feel the water, really *luxuriate*—this time is just for you. Stand or sit for 10 minutes, just feeling the warmth of the water, the soft flow, on your skin. Focus your thoughts on the feeling. Breathe deeply, and let the water wash your anxieties and running thoughts away.

For an added benefit, create a detox bath. Mix 1 cup of Epsom salts with ½ cup of baking soda, and add to your bath water. You can drop a few drops of therapeutic grade essential oils in, too. Try clary sage or frankincense to detoxify, and lavender, ylang ylang, or vetiver to relax more deeply.

How did spending time with water feel? Did the water lessen the stress you may have been feeling prior? Did it help you relax more?

_____

_____

_____

_____

_____

_____

_____

_____

_____

_____

_____

_____

_____

_____

_____

_____

_____

_____

Day 17

When we can be fully in the present moment, everything amplifies. Some people try to escape the present moment because it doesn't always feel good. We live in a culture overrun with escapism. Media and entertainment helps us escape. Addiction, whether to substances, situations, relationships, or experiences, is a significant distraction to entice us and prevent us from being fully present to reality. When we try to shape the future or escape the past, we can miss the present moment where peace and tranquility live. I hope this exercise helps you see the escapism and take steps to avoid it.

Escapism prolongs suffering and keeps you from developing a full, rich life. Your body will still feel stress, even if you've tricked your mind into pushing it away. By being present for difficult situations, you move through them with greater and greater skill, developing courage and strength you never imagined possible.

- How do you avoid the present moment when it feels stressful? How can you be more present to the moment? Would being present change the situation? Could it change the outcome?

Day 18

We have a tremendous opportunity to immerse ourselves in ecstatic joy. In this meditation, you will fly, visualizing yourself as a bird or the pilot of a tiny jet built just for you.

In this meditation, you'll experience a sensation that may feel odd at first, but keep flying. Choose a path you take often, such as the way to school or work. Rise up in your mind, and hover over your house. Now take off. As landmarks come into view, do you see anything you've always missed in your travels? Do you see anything new?

- Describe how you imagined your flight. Did you take note of something you had never looked at carefully before? Did you notice something new as if by magic? Could you conjure a sense of freedom?

Day 19

Sometimes the belief in the goodness and benevolence of life can lead to a sense of peace. At times, this benevolence is striking and sudden and can feel like a miracle. The miracles I speak of can be as simple as finding lost family heirlooms or getting a job in the field you've dreamt of joining. Miracles are all around you if you just slow down enough to look; a widow finds love again, a lost pet returns, a child takes her first steps. As you grow quiet and surrender to the world around you, you'll experience them too. Sometimes an unlikely occurrence precedes a miracle, and sometimes that occurrence is negative. By exploring this deeper, you might come to understand that that negative event led to something so positive and powerful that it seems like a miracle. Surrender to the idea something else is at work in your life, that miracle energy.

This is an invitation and an opportunity to step deeply into the *art of allowing*. Be receptive and invite the energy of our benevolent universe into your life. Give in to the flow. The spectacular wants to exist in your presence and shape your life. Let it, and watch the miraculous bloom all around you.

- What are some examples of these benevolent moments in your life? Were they specific events? Or a feeling?

Day 20

We all have challenges to surmount in our lives. What is stressing you the most? Make a list and, using the tools you've learned, reassess it. If your top problem is money for rent, list how you used the money and acknowledge it. Don't run from reality. Close your eyes, and breathe deeply. Open your eyes, and work on solutions.

- Journal about your stressors here. Can you acknowledge them clearly and without judgment? Can you use the light to move through difficulty and advocate for yourself and what you love? Can your mind find innovative solutions?

Day 21

Today, we will practice a meditation. We will use a mantra to help keep our minds focused on something simple instead of listening to the running commentary in our brains provided by our inner narrator.

Repeat the words *shri ram*, and sit quietly for about 5 minutes. This mantra brings a sense of confidence and success to your being. Whenever your mind wanders, repeat your mantra again. This Sanskrit mantra is inspired by the Hindu deity Rama, who was described as successful and victorious; the words mean "victorious Rama."

- How do you feel after that meditation session? Rested? Refreshed? Or something else? Write about it. Did you get a sense of your inner victorious self?

Day 22

Human beings have the amazing ability to feel as if something is happening simply by imagining it. When you simply imagine doing something, your body produces many of the chemicals that would've been released had we actually done the activity.

In this exercise, we'll use our imaginations to find a moment of calm. Envision yourself in a lush, green forest walking down a path. Rays of sunlight stream through gaps in the tree branches. You can see wildflowers dotted here and there. You feel a sense of peace in this forest. It is a safe place that is full of life.

As you walk through the forest, notice the trees. How big are they? What does the bark look like? What do their leaves look like? Envision yourself walking over to one of those trees and sitting with your back against it. The tree is firm and supportive. The ground is soft and covered by a cozy layer of fresh green moss. Rest and lean back into the tree. Breathe in the fresh air.

How did it feel to imagine this walk through a forest? What did you notice? How did your visualization compare to the real-life experience of a walk in nature?

Day 23

When we reach out to others, we care for ourselves and the universe. Isolation can make you feel that you are the only one facing problems and uncertainties. It's not true; we all have many of the same worries.

Contact and communication—visiting and taking care of others—help you move your focus from excessive rumination and negative thoughts. By just calling a friend and listening, you can step outside of yourself and help another—and that person just might just help you. Look around. Does the neighbor need yard work? Is there a child that needs some company? The world is a big place and can use your help.

Today, reach out to one person in your life. Call, write, or drop by. Connect, help, and get involved. The more you interact with the people in your life, community, and world, the more peace you will find inside.

- Make a list of people you want to contact and reach out to. What happened? How do you feel?

Day 24

Today, let's relieve some tension and stretch out your lower lumbar region and your hamstrings with the "legs-up-the-wall" yoga pose. Stretching is a huge part of yoga. It calms and relaxes while helping your body become supple and flexible. Tension can be common in the lower back, and whether you work with your hands, chase children, or lift groceries, this stretch can relieve the tension. You'll also diminish pain, another stressor.

You can choose to do this easy, restful yoga posture on the floor or on a bed with a headboard. Lie down as close to the wall or headboard as you can; if you need to lie down a few inches away, that is fine. Turn and position yourself so that the backs of your legs are flat against the wall. You want your legs to rest up against the wall at about a ninety-degree angle. Extend your arms out in a T shape. Relax and breathe deeply. Enjoy this posture for five to twenty minutes. If you fall asleep and stay in this position longer, that's okay, too. When you are ready to come out of it, you can bring the bottoms of your feet together, like a butterfly, rest that way for a few minutes, and then slide them down the wall and roll to your side to sit up.

- How do you feel after that respite? Write about what you notice.

Day 25

Our sense of calm is often threatened by anger. In this visualization exercise, you will provide a release valve to these feelings and as a result free up space for greater peace and calm. Find a secluded area where you can be unobserved and preferably a little bit loud. Start in a standing position. Breathe deeply into your abdomen, and begin to stomp your feet. On your next big inhale, envision the breath coming into you; when you exhale sharply, visualize it exiting your solar plexus and forming a storm cloud in front of your body. Continue breathing, and visualize an increase in the size of the storm cloud.

Inhale deeply and then with a forceful exhalation, imagine a bolt of lightning coming out of the storm cloud and striking the Earth. With each lightning strike, you release any pent-up anger. You can also clap your hands, shout, and stomp your feet. Repeat at least twenty times and keep snapping lighting down into the earth. Allow yourself to truly let go and release the feelings within you. You may not know what they are all about. That's okay. Afterward, let your breathing return to normal, and take a few moments to sit down and wrap your arms around yourself and give yourself a hug.

- What did you notice when you completed the exercise? How do you feel now?

Day 26

Today, we'll complete an exercise called "watching the breath." The flow of air in and out of the lungs is tied directly to the amount of oxygen and energy that travels through your body. By focusing on your breath, you give your body a short holiday that refreshes the mind and fills it with energizing oxygen.

Find a comfortable position lying on your back, sitting down cross-legged, or sitting in a chair with both feet grounded on the floor. Gently exhale all the breath from your lungs through your nose, emptying the lungs completely. As you inhale, follow your breath with your awareness. Notice how the breath flows in through the nostrils and down into the lungs and how your body expands. When you exhale, notice how the breath leaves the body and the lungs empty.

Begin to create a three-part yogic breath. First fill the belly, then move the breath up to fill the rib cage and thoracic area, and then allow the chest to rise and fill with air. Exhale completely in the reverse order. First empty the chest, then the ribcage, and then the belly. Continue these three-part yogic breaths, while keeping your attention on the sensations you are experiencing.

Allow yourself to just be. Your only task is to breathe with awareness. Each time you notice your mind wandering, bring your awareness back to each inhalation and exhalation.

⬤ What did you notice as you paid attention to your breathing? Do you now feel a sense of stillness? Do your thoughts seem more focused?

Day 27

Insight meditation, which involves using your awareness to observe your thoughts, can inspire you and improve your health by reducing levels of stress and anxiety, helping you get more restful sleep. (Some Buddhists believe that deep insight meditation can even serve as the path to enlightenment!) The key to this type of meditation is a nonjudgmental attitude. You may think your thoughts are uninteresting. Believe me, when it comes to your life, they are not. As you observe your thoughts, do not evaluate or judge yourself for the things that cross your mind. Do not attach yourself or your identity to the thoughts that pass by. You'll soon find yourself slowing down your thinking and reducing mental chatter, helping to quiet your mind.

Try this now for about ten minutes. Start with deep breathing. Use each breath as an opportunity to anchor your mind back into the present. If your mind is wandering already, focus on inhaling and exhaling. Don't resist any thoughts that come up. Simply observe them, and allow them to float by. You are curious about them, but not attached to them. Notice the stillness that may arrive in the space between the thoughts.

- What thoughts did you observe?

- How did your experience with this meditation change your mental chatter?

Day 28

Now, take stock of your immediate surroundings. Where in your home do you feel the calmest? Where is your happy place? Do you have more than one? Do you need to create one, a corner of the house with soft pillows and candlelight? Now think of a wider area. Can you be in nature? Is there water? Can you visit a park or garden? Are there spots to visit and practice what you've learned?

- Make of list of all the easily accessible places where you feel comfortable and calm. Write down your thoughts about each place. You can refer to these pages later and use this list to take yourself to a happy place.

Day 29

Today, all you have to do is listen to music. Scientists still do not know all of the parts of the brain that are affected by music. Some suspect that the entire organ appreciates music and helps create it. Others argue that our love of music is a leftover part of our evolution; we once made music to communicate.

Whatever you believe, listening to music has been proven to lower cortisol levels (the hormone that's released when you're stressed) and calm the mind. Truly listening creates a singular focus not unlike a visualization exercise; it's a mini vacation for the mind.

Find a comfortable spot, and turn on some music. Choose a song that makes you feel light, airy, upbeat, relaxed. Music can evoke feelings so easily. Try 20 minutes of classical music, light jazz, or ballads. In this case, you want to focus on music, not words. Begin deep breathing, and listen to the sound.

- List the music you chose. How did you feel when you listened?

Day 30

Cultivating a compassionate, kind, and patient voice within ourselves can yield a better quality of life. When we are nicer to ourselves and more accepting of our shortcomings, this feeling of openness and understanding ripples out to the world around us.

Compassion makes us feel good. It activates the pleasure circuits in our brain, yet we can find it so difficult to be kind to ourselves. Kindness, including kindness toward the self, makes us less prone to heart disease. It lowers stress hormones. Brain scans done during loving-kindness meditation show that the mind wanders less and, as a result, we feel happier and less angry with others.

Answer these questions to show you the way toward practicing self-compassion.

- What do I need? What do I already have?

- When and how was I overly critical of myself, especially when it was unimportant?

- Do I criticize myself over and over about the same things? What are they?

Day 31

In the stress, wild rushing, and general busyness of modern life, we don't pause long enough to acknowledge the good that comes into our lives every day.

In this exercise, think about your day and list every kindness shown to you by a loved one, colleague, friend, neighbor, or stranger. It can be as simple as a big smile that cheered you up or a coworker commending your work to the boss. Did you get great service at the garage? Did the cashier at the grocery recommend sale items?

- List the moments of kindness that you experienced today.

- How did each one make you feel?

Day 32

Feeling safe is an important part of calm. The more focused your mind is, the safer you'll feel as you confront challenges and make decisions. The less you allow negative or distorted images and information to fill your screen, the safer you will feel.

When facing stressful situations, imagining places of safety is a great way to center your thoughts. Today, you'll list where you feel safest. You can write anything from your parents' house and summer camp to a state of mind, such as playing music with your friends. You can also write a description of your "safe spot," where you can live and work in complete calm. Revisit your list from time to time to keep it fresh in your mind. When you feel stress, conjure up the images of these places as you breathe deeply.

- List or describe the places that you feel safest. Write about each place with as much detail as possible, creating a clear picture in your mind.

Day 33

Habits are behaviors that you do over and over. Some habits are unconscious, whereas others are created through choice. Perhaps you take 10 minutes to meditate every night before bed. That's a conscious habit. You may also drum your fingers on the table when you are nervous. That too is a habit, albeit unconscious. In this exercise, we'll focus on the conscious habits that calm you.

Your mind can be trained in the same way a major league pitcher trains his arm—through repetition. Every time you complete a certain activity, your brain's thought patterns change. You can access calm anywhere just by repeating your calming habits.

- First, create a list of what calms you. Is it a warm bath? Needlepoint? Walking? Playing music? Dancing? Underneath each activity, describe how you feel both before and after completing the calming action.

- How often do you partake in these calming habits? Are you consistently giving yourself time to de-stress every day? Do you need to build up your calming habits, creating more time to recharge and care for yourself?

- After your list is complete and your feelings noted, consider all the exercises you've done up until this one. Can you fold one of them into your day and make it into a calming habit?

Day 34

When you were young, you could pass days doing nothing but playing and relaxing. As we grow and take on more responsibility, the days of play grow fewer and fewer. But slowing down is important. Even adults need to have some fun. By taking a moment to do nothing and have fun, not only will life feel richer, you'll lower your heart rate and blood pressure, keeping you healthier in the long run.

When you literally stop to smell the flowers, you rejuvenate yourself as well as those around you. Playing with a child, walking a dog, or hanging out with a friend creates calming feelings; taking moments to pause and exchange helps you relax and enjoy the feelings of connecting with other beings. Sometimes, not getting something done is better than rushing through your obligations.

- Look at your to-do list. Is there anything that can wait until tomorrow? Is everything about your life a rush, or can you slow certain parts down? Can you create a space in your day to just be?

- After you identify this space, list the ways you'd like to spend that time. Can you make it happen? If you did, how would it make you feel?

Day 35

Every point of contact with another being is an exchange, sometimes pleasing and sometimes not. As humans, we often give the "sometimes not" people far too much headspace while taking for granted the supportive people in our lives. One step in creating a calmer life is being mindful of the type of energy each person in your life presents to you, as well as what you offer to others.

Today, we'll focus on the good people who bring you great energy and light. It's important to keep supportive loving people close and make it an ongoing conscious effort to reach out them. Investing time in these individuals always pays off; it's a gift.

- Make a list of the family, friends, neighbors, and colleagues who consistently provide you with positive support and encouragement.

- Ask yourself what you provide to them in return. How often do you reach out? Should you do it more often?

- Then select one person to whom you would like to write a note of appreciation or to give a call. Tell them what their friendship and kind words have meant to you over the years. If this person inspires you, share that with them as well.

Day 36

This simple visualization exercise helps you practice conjuring relaxing feelings and visions when you're stressed.

Relax in a comfortable place. Imagine you're sitting in a desert or on the beach with sand beneath your feet. Notice what scene is more compelling to you. Do you enjoy the hot, dry, and loose dirt of the desert or the calmness of a beach? No matter your choice, feel your feet on the sand. Wiggle your toes and feet, and dig them down deeper into the sand until you've immersed your feet up over your ankles. How would it feel to have your feet in the sand, in the Earth? Imagine what it might feel like.

- Write about your experience with this exercise. Describe how that connection to the warm sand feels, and see if you can maintain it throughout the day.

Day 37

For today's daily dose of calm, we will explore the world of color. Take a moment, and think about a feeling of serenity. What colors symbolize that feeling of tranquility for you? Perhaps it's a pastel blue, lavender, buttermilk yellow, a fresh light green, or white. Try different colors in your awareness. Aqua blue, turquoise, plum, violet, pale pink, rose gold, bright pink, light yellow, sunflower yellow, peach, tangerine. Now envision emerald green, fresh apple green, and mint green.

- Let the range of colors run wild in your mind, and make a list of the colors you visualized. Under each color, write how it made you feel. What colors did you choose, and which ones felt the most calming to you? Which colors felt joyful? Which energized you?

- Can you list ways you can include them into your environment? For example, can you surround yourself with those serene colors in your home and environment by painting a wall with the calming color or, for a smaller project, by applying the color to a bedside table or picture frame? How about finding a sweater, hat, lipstick, or mug in your "happy" hues?

Day 38

If you keep your thoughts moving and let some of them go, you are more likely to keep a sense of serenity and avoid getting stuck on worries. Allow yourself to feel like all is right with the world with the help of this meditation.

Imagine yourself lying on a soft, comfortable blanket. You are looking up at a blue sky dotted with clouds. These clouds are fluffy and bright white. Enjoy the way they look. Watch these passing clouds in your mind and how they interact with the sunlight. When a thought arises, send it to one of the clouds and watch it float away. Keep your attention on watching these moving clouds, and if a worry or concern or a to-do list item surfaces, send it up on one of those clouds and watch it. Watch it be blown away on that gentle breeze.

- What worries or thoughts did you allow to float away? Do any of them come back? If so, you can list them.

Day 39

Enter into deep calmness using one of your most powerful tools: your imagination. Sit in a meditative posture. You can lie down, sit with your hands in your lap, or in any meditation pose that feels good to you. Whether it's day or night, imagine yourself sitting or lying outside in a beautiful landscape bathed in moonlight. What does this moonlit landscape look like to you? Is the moon full? Are there stars in the sky? Are you on grass, dirt, or sand? What is the scenery like here? Enjoy this beautiful setting. Rest in this place as you're meditating mindfully, noticing your surroundings, and repeat the word bliss in your mind. This feeling of bliss, this mix of happiness and serenity, is coming to you now. Continue to repeat the word as you meditate.

- Write about the word *bliss*. What does it mean to you?

- How did this nighttime scene feel? What did you picture? Is it a real place, and could you go there one night?

Day 40

So many minutes of our lives are spent worrying about the future and what might happen next. Will things go the way that I would like with my job? Will I be safe? Will I be cared for over the years? Many of our worries are survival based, but instead of projecting into the future, what might letting go of worry feel like?

Today, set an intention to let go of your worries. If any worries arise at any point of the day, let them surface without judgment. Write the worry down, and begin to imagine a breeze ruffling your paper. Experience this breeze like a gentle gust of wind. Hear the sound it makes as it passes your ears, and allow any of your worry about the future to fly away. You can even discard the paper in the trash to take the process of letting go of your worries even further.

- In this journal, write out each worry followed by a description of your feelings watching it blow away. After you have completed this first "worry" list, repeat this exercise a couple times a week or whenever your worries build and create anxiety and pressure inside of you.

Day 41

One of the emotions that we tend to store and avoid is fear. A lot of us even disassociate from our fears because, well, fear is scary. Fear that is stored in our body can tie up and divert energy that can be put to another positive use. Today, we will release some of this fear.

Sit for a moment, and place the tip of your tongue behind your two front teeth. This helps bring the two hemispheres of your brain into greater harmony. This will make it easier for you to let go of fear with ease and grace.

With your tongue behind your two front teeth, write a list of your fears on a piece of paper. Under each, describe how the fear makes you feel and then ask yourself these questions.

- Is this fear real? Can I see it or touch it? Is it an immediate threat or a free-floating fear about your life, your family, or the world in general? Can you take action to lessen the threat and therefore lessen the fear? (In most instances, you can accomplish this by turning off the news!)

- How did you feel as you wrote this list down? Did you notice any physical sensations?

Day 42

Today, you will connect with your higher self. This is the part of you that is infinite and all-knowing. Imagine yourself walking down a path made of evenly spaced, beautifully textured stepping stones. Each stone leads to the next, and all you need to do is put one foot in front of the other to step on each successive stone. As you take these steps, discover a feeling of peace within you. Notice how each stone looks. What color is it? How does it feel when your foot touches the stone? Is your foot bare?

Use your imagination to visualize a focused image of you stepping on the beautiful path that is laid out before you. This path is just for you. It's the path that you have created using your free will. It's a beautiful path. Notice how the stones are just right for you. As you continue this visualization, notice your thoughts slowing down, feel your mind clear, and allow yourself to be in the flow of life.

Write about how it felt to focus on stepping from stone to stone. What does the concept of your higher self mean to you? Do you feel comfortable trusting that part of you? Explore these thoughts, feelings, and ideas.

Day 43

What are the three essentials in your life? Food, water, and shelter should not be on your list; the essentials that we're talking about here are ones that speak to your values, what you care about, what you want in life, and what matters to you.

Identifying these three essentials helps you create the life you want. Knowing what you want makes it easier to achieve what you desire in your life. Clarity of purpose also creates calm, as you know the important elements of your life that you need to develop and protect. Each time you're faced with a tough decision, ask yourself if that choice supports your intentions, and the answer to this question will help you choose.

- Write down those three essentials. What are the first things that come to mind? If your list says "caring for my family," "caring for myself," and "caring for my community," your decisions should revolve around those three things.

- Next, create two affirmative statements: one about taking action to put those essentials in place in your life in the way you like, and one about receiving and attracting those with ease. Keep these affirmations and essentials at the forefront in your mind as you make your decisions.

Day 44

Today, you will enter your inner heart's temple. It is a healing place where your energy lives. Take a deep breath, and bring your attention to the center of your chest. Visualize yourself in miniature walking through a door into the center of your own chest, into the room of your heart.

Look around. You are in a foyer. How is it decorated? What color is it? Is it well lit? Does the foyer please you? If not, you can add lighting and decorations to your liking. Simply think of it, and it will appear. Perhaps you add sparkling crystal chandeliers and fresh flowers on beautiful tables. Perhaps you change the color of the walls. Think about what would feel good. Are there candles or golden statuettes? Walk deeper through the foyer and into a great room. The ceilings are very high, and the room is incredibly spacious. How is it decorated? Once again, you may redecorate as you choose.

Notice that there are many hallways and doors off of this room. They contain everything to bring you joy and to make your heart feel good. Allow yourself to explore this space.

● Describe your room. What did it look like? Did it feel relaxing in there?

Day 45

Give your mind a break by letting your imagination run free. Do you have a favorite animal? Is there an animal that you associate with yourself? (For example, I was always a fan of the blue whale, even as a child.) If you don't have a favorite animal, do you have a pet? Did you have one as a child?

Next, think about this animal and what it means to you. Then, imagine how it would feel to be this animal. If you could have the powerful presence of a wild mustang, would you feel more capable? If you could embody the beautiful iridescence of a dragonfly, would you feel more in touch with the magic of everyday life?

- What animal did you choose? What did the animal mean for you?

- What other animals would you like to try this exercise with? Make a list.

Day 46

Today, we will turn your worries into positive goals that inspire you to accomplish more without insecurity and fear. This is a tool that you can revisit as you bring more calm to your life.

Instead of rising with a negative thought, "I am never getting this project done," flip your point of view to "this project gives me a chance to conquer and shine." If a negative thought enters your head, flip it immediately into a positive; you have everything you need to power through this day.

You have the innate power within you to alchemize your life through conscious attention; now you will do this with your worries. When faced with a negative thought such as "I can never get the laundry done," how might you flip it? "I'll do the wash, spreading it over two days. That gives me a rest, and I get clean clothes" is one example. Another positive spin might be "I could catch up on my reading" or "That's the time I can work on reports." In other words, take what you perceive as lemons and make lemonade.

○ To focus, write down a specific aspect of your life that troubles you repeatedly. How do you feel when you reread what you've written? Now flip it; turn the negative into a positive opportunity.

Day 47

For a few minutes today, slip into a peaceful pocket within yourself. Your peaceful pocket can be literal as in a favorite soft sofa or a corner of a yard or garden; it can also be an activity such as a quick walk, closing your eyes for 10 minutes, or a hot bath. You can envision any image in your mind. Lean back into yourself and imagine the moment mindfully with no judgment and complete acceptance. Feel yourself sit back within your being and melt into rest and calmness. Breathe deeply. Visualize that you're bringing your breath all the way down to your toes; feel them tingle. Repeat this deep, slow breathing.

Bring the intention of your breathing all the way to the bottoms of your feet. Allow the idea of mindful presence to seep into your consciousness. There's nothing for you to do. Just read these words: "There is nothing I have to do in this moment except just be." Feel that detached, yet unconditionally loving presence within you. Breathe and witness your being. Stay this way for a few minutes.

- When you're done, journal about your experience. What images did you picture?

Day 48

Your body holds tension, and that tension can be a symptom of stress, an impediment to good health and happiness. Not only does that tension indicate stress, it causes physical pain that detracts from your sense of peace.

Movement—gentle stretching or a short walk—can help mentally and physically unknot the tension that arises throughout the day. If your shoulders are rising toward your ears, roll them forward and backward for a few moments as you breathe in and out deeply. If your legs ache, find a private spot and stretch, bending at the waist and reaching your hands to your toes. Your hamstrings and the backs of your legs should release what they are holding. If your head aches, try walking while taking deep breaths of fresh air. When your day is ending, exercise or a long hot bath can further alleviate tension.

- Throughout the day, take a moment to survey your body, and learn where stress lives in your body. Is it in your neck? Tired shoulders? Tight legs or sore feet? How does your body feel? Make a list of where stress lives in your body.

- What did you do to unravel it? How did you feel afterward?

Day 49

Serotonin is a chemical in the brain that brings calm to the mind and balance to the multiple systems in the body. It's released by nerve cells in your digestive tract, and its production can be amped up and down with food. The more serotonin-rich food you eat, the calmer you should feel. Other chemicals that help you feel good are endorphins. These chemicals behave like opioids, blocking pain and stress. They are responsible for pleasure and are stimulated and released through exercise, massage, and bodywork.

To boost your serotonin levels, select low-glycemic natural carbohydrates like sweet potatoes and garbanzo beans. Other serotonin-promoting foods include pineapple, tofu, salmon, spinach, nuts, turkey, eggs, and seeds. For endorphin-inspiring, feel-good foods, try chocolate, chili peppers, berries, grapes, ginseng, seeds, nuts, and vanilla.

Endorphins are also released through massage, exercise, sex, laughter, acupuncture, and meditation. Ten minutes of yoga will release endorphins and powerful anti-aging chemicals. A brisk walk or taking a couple flights of stairs quickly will also give you a short boost. To create a sustained, peaceful flow of endorphins, set up a regular exercise routine.

- Use the information to think about different ways to promote the release of serotonin and endorphins. Make a list of what you would like to try.

Day 50

When we practice mindfulness, we open ourselves up to all of our emotions. In this exercise, you will observe these emotions without judgment. This might seem scary, especially when it means we may experience less pleasant emotions more deeply. Many of us spend lots of time and effort to avoid these emotions; feelings that are too overwhelming, too frightening, and too intense make us want to place our attention elsewhere.

In this sense, mindfulness is an act of great courage. It is an understanding that we actually control very little and have the opportunity to be fully aware of the complexity and duality of the life we are living. We have a chance in this life to immerse ourselves in the experience of being human with all of its ups and downs, twists and turns. It is part of the dance of being human. While we dance that dance, we can find greater calm if we bring awareness and mindfulness to our beings.

How willing are you to be deeply present in each moment, pleasant and unpleasant? How mindful have you been in past situations? Can you list a specific situation where, had you been completely present, the outcome might have been different?

Day 51

A body scan is an intensely relaxing visualization. If you've taken a yoga class, a body scan often makes up the last act, giving you the chance to return your body to your consciousness completely. With a body scan, you can stay in touch with your entire physical being, feeling grounded and whole. In fact, many people feel so grounded that they don't want to get up! This calming practice can also help you get to sleep.

Lie on your back with your arms stretched out to the sides, palms up. Turn your attention to the soles of your feet, focusing completely on how they feel. Move up to your ankles. Pause to really consider how they feel. Continue slowly to calves, knees, thighs, and your entire body until you reach the crown of your head. Pause for a few moments at each body part. Every time you move your focus, imagine light and energy flowing into the spaces inside of you; this awareness may feel like a pulsing or a tingling.

- How did your body scan feel? Did your limbs tingle or become warm? Did you feel yourself sinking into the floor? As you became more present to your body, did you experience a sense of peace?

Day 52

Learning how to forgive yourself can bring you a sense of peace. Forgiveness opens you to the light when darkness falls over your life and lets you avoid any distracting and obsessive negative energy.

None of us is perfect; we all have actions in our past that do not make us proud. The point is to be aware of these actions and continue to grow from them. Ditch the idea of perfection and embrace the idea of moving through your days with grace. Reflecting on these actions brings awareness, and once aware, you can forgive yourself. You can acknowledge that there might be better ways to approach a situation.

We are often our own worst critics. Our inner perfectionist might focus disproportionately on a relatively small mistake. For example, a few years ago, I told some close friends something I had heard about two acquaintances. It was about a loud public fight that they had in their yard. Immediately after I said it, I felt terrible. I didn't want to gossip and wished I hadn't mentioned it. For weeks after, I would think of that moment and cringe. Even now, writing about it, I still wish I'd made a different choice.

● Write about a moment where you hurt others, even in a small way. Describe the action and then re-create the thinking beneath the action. For example, if your action is taking the car when you knew someone needed it, ask yourself the following questions: *Why did you take the car? Was the need true? Did you need it or just didn't want this person to have it? Were you angry about something else when you took the car?* Be as honest as possible about your intentions.

_____

_____

_____

_____

_____

_____

_____

_____

_____

_____

_____

_____

_____

_____

_____

_____

_____

_____

Day 53

Awareness of the world around you grounds the mind and calms the soul. Today, you will turn your awareness to everyday sensory pleasures. You might find that they add a depth and richness to your life that you might not have believed possible.

Your senses bring you tastes, smells, touch, and images that can enrich and enliven. Imagine sensations you love; this can be anything from "hot water hitting my skin" to "the smell of fresh pie." Do you have a favorite soft blanket you wrap yourself in? Can you imagine how it feels? Simple pleasures, such as a sun-drenched catnap or noticing the breeze as it caresses your skin, will allow you to relax and feel more nourished by daily life.

- List at least 10 of these sensations in your journal, and see if you can experience at least one of them every day for the next 10 days. Your list can include the ideas listed above and others that you create. If you've been experiencing more everyday stress lately, you might want to add more to the list and provide yourself with extra self-care and enjoyment.

Day 54

The warmth of the sun feels so lovely on a summer morning. When the sun hits your skin, it interacts with the cholesterol in your skin to create vitamin D, the anti-depression vitamin. Its brightness and light nourish the spirit. The sun is your quickest mood booster when you feel irritable, and it's an express train to calm.

A short sunbath in the middle of a stressful day can return you to a sense of centered calm. Try adding 10 minutes of sun to your day, building up to 20 minutes, if you can. Find a quiet spot, feel the sun on your skin, and breathe in and out deeply. Feel the oxygen energize your blood while the sun's warmth soothes your skin. Let the magic chemistry of the natural world happen, as you manufacture your own feel-good vitamins. The more skin you expose to the sun, the more your skin can soak it up and turn it into vitamin D. Your upper back is the most potent place for the vitamin D from sunlight to be absorbed, so if you can expose this part of the body to the sun, all the better. To best absorb your vitamin D, refrain from washing the sunlit skin for six hours. Let nature's innate medicine cabinet increase your well-being. (Only do this if you are able to spend this time in the sun without sunscreen and not get a sunburn.)

- Bring your journal outside, and write about how the sun makes you feel. Your thoughts don't need to be polished. Just describe what you experience.

Day 55

Extraordinary happiness and beauty is woven through ordinary life if you slow down long enough to observe the world. See warmth in the eyes of a stranger. Notice the laughter of children in the street or the beautiful line of a building you never noticed before. Appreciate the smile you shared with the store clerk. Witness the drops of rain as they hit the pavement. Enjoy the smell of that shower, the sound of the drops percussing on the asphalt. The moment is beautiful. To witness this endless beauty, all you need do is be mindfully present; slow the world down and savor what you see, hear, smell, and feel like a delicious meal.

If you turn your focus to these countless moments of beauty rather than on unpleasant thoughts, you anchor yourself to the bounty of the universe, the glorious flow. Your soul calms as you come to believe and rely on a kind world presenting you with countless wonders. Are you excited to think about what you might see tomorrow?

> List all the beauty that you experienced today. How did it make you feel? Did you notice new aspects of your world that you didn't before?

Day 56

One aspect of a centered calm life is knowing your limits. We all have people we hate to let down. We all say yes too, even when we're too tired or need to recharge. We continually drive ourselves to do just one more thing. Our reasons are endless. You think "If I don't go to the party, I'll never get invited again!" or "My partner is going to scream if I don't pick up the dry cleaning, but it's across town!" The "one more thing" generates big stress.

Ask yourself what would happen if you stayed home. Could you send a kind note and a gift instead? If you explain your exhaustion to your partner and commit to picking up the dry cleaning tomorrow, would there really be yelling? People tend to be more kind and forgiving than you might think. Give it a chance.

- Write down a recent experience where you stretched yourself too far.

- Why did you do it? Did you believe something unpleasant would happen if you took a step back and took care of your needs?

- When you honored your needs, how did those around you react? Was it what you expected, or were you surprised?

Day 57

As we look at all the ways that you can find a sense of peace and calm, don't underestimate the power of deep breathing. The air that you pull into your body and the oxygen that you deliver to your brain, your organs, and your muscles are life-giving. When you become stressed and threatened, you hold your breath, literally starving your body of energy when it needs it most. You might hold your breath when you see something beautiful or become excited. You can even hold your breath during workouts!

Today's exercise will help you develop awareness of your breath so that you can understand your breathing. Inhale into your abdomen, then ribcage, and then upper chest. Imagine you are filling a paper bag from bottom to top. Next, exhale slowly from top to bottom, drawing the exhalation out. You might want to exhale through your mouth, nose, or pursed lips. See what feels good. Try all three variations and explore how long you can make each exhalation. Be completely immersed in "watching" the breath. Continue the breathing cycle for at least 3 to 5 minutes.

○ How did your body feel as you engaged in this conscious deep breathing? Does anything tingle? Does your body feel warm?

Day 58

By now, you've built a lot of expertise at finding calm. You'll add to this expertise with a yoga nidra, also known as "yogic sleep." This ancient practice allows you to access the restorative powers of sleep without actually sleeping. Some studies have shown that 20 minutes of yoga nidra is equivalent to 2 to 3 hours of restful sleep, providing deep rest when your demanding schedule puts a short nap out of reach. This particular sequence of body awareness combined with visualization of various outdoor scenes causes a down-regulation in your nervous system, unwinding tension in your body.

Lie down in a comfortable position, making sure that you do not feel any tension in your body. Close your eyes. Set your intention to finding your calm center.

Begin by bringing your attention to the center of your forehead, between your brows; you may feel a pulsing sensation. Next, bring your attention to the center of your chest. Notice how this feels. Bring your attention to your right palm, then return it to the center of your chest. Do the same with your left palm. Move your awareness to your navel, down to the right knee, then the ball of your right foot, back up to your knee, and back to your navel.

Now move your awareness to your left knee. Next, on down to the ball of your left foot. Circle back up to your left knee, then your navel, the center of your chest, and finally your brow center.

Next, quickly and with little thought, picture a windswept beach, then a city skyline, next a verdant forest, and last a nighttime sky.

How did that feel? Did you enjoy a sense of relaxation as you brought your attention to different parts of your body and pictured the different scenes? Write about this.

_____

_____

_____

_____

_____

_____

_____

_____

_____

_____

_____

_____

_____

_____

_____

_____

Day 59

The potential for something in your life to cause stress is all around. Sometimes, the car won't start. Other days, it rains when you are having an outdoor party, or road construction takes you 15 minutes out of your way and makes you a half hour late. The world is full of these moments.

But there is another kind of stress—the kind you may put on yourself. You may be a perfectionist, not wanting to let go of a report until you've read it 15 times. You may have set a ridiculous goal that is impossible to attain. You may have heard of catch-phrases such as "first million by 25" or "write the great American novel by 30." Well, who says? Every life is different. Be uniquely you. Stand out. Shine. The world needs your prismatic soul. Would your life be over if you didn't make junior partner by next year? What about 5 years from now? Give yourself the respect and freedom to accomplish your dreams whenever they come into your life.

- List the self-imposed expectations that cause you stress. Explain why you believe you must achieve these things. How can you change these expectations?

- Next, write about who you are. Avoid listing your accomplishments. Explain why you are wonderful. Contemplate the ways in which your self-worth should be tied to who you are rather than what you produce.

Day 60

Writing down your thoughts is another effective way of infusing calm into a stressful day; it makes you pause and unpack what happened. For instance, say your day felt unusually stressful, even by your standards. You ran late in the morning. The boss was unhappy. What happened when the boss confronted you? How was the remainder of your day? Did this event color your mood for everything else that happened?

On the flip side, say that you had a wonderful day. You may have gotten a new job and gone shopping for new work clothes. You feel great, like you are starting a fresh, new chapter of your life. How exciting! Journaling about your happy feelings can also help you reflect. For example, you may ask yourself if you can handle the goodness of the universe while keeping humility and love at your side.

- What happened today? How did you feel about it?

- If you had a stressful day, how could you have relieved some of the stress? Could you have done anything differently to change the outcome? Write down your answers in a nonjudgmental fashion. Your goal is to express how you feel and learn from today, not re-create negativity.

Day 61

A shortcut to joy is laughter. When you laugh, your brain releases endorphins, those feel-good chemicals we discussed earlier on page 104, and dopamine, perhaps the ultimate feel-good chemical. When these naturally occurring chemicals are released into your bloodstream, they bring pleasure and calmness, lower your blood pressure, and help you sleep. Just as meditation and deep breathing can halt negative circular thoughts that cause depression, so can laughter.

Here, we'll introduce this wonderful stress-reliever into your day. Your task is to simply spend 10 minutes with a person who makes you laugh. You can also watch animal videos or your favorite comic. Allow yourself to smile, chuckle, and laugh from the belly as much as you want. Got a tough job with little humor? Befriend a colleague who makes you smile so that at least you'll have a partner in joy to visit throughout stressful days. Keep your favorite channel of funny videos at the ready; you can grab a short 2-minute chuckle from time to time. Smile—it, too, releases endorphins!

- **List all the people and things that make you laugh.**
  Can you access them easily during the course of your day?

Day 62

On this day, you'll need a candle. Most homes have them for safety or ambience. Here, you'll focus on the flame and meditate. Many people find this meditation easier than working with mantras.

Sit in a comfortable position in a slightly darkened room. Block out as much noise as you can; you are seeking to be alone with just the flame. Place your candle at eye level or just slightly below it. Light the candle.

For the next 10 minutes, focus on nothing but the flame. Is it steady, or does it move? As you stare at the flame, does it appear to shine brighter or softer? If thoughts arise and take your attention off the flame, acknowledge them without judgment and return to the flame.

- After 10 minutes have passed, blow out your candle and describe how you felt during your candle meditation. How do you feel after completing it? If you continue to explore this exercise, experiment with candles that emit aromatherapy smells: lavender for sleep; rosemary, lemon, or pine for energy; and chamomile or rose for anxiety. Be sure to use clean-burning beeswax or soy candles.

Day 63

In this visualization exercise, imagine yourself walking in a sunlit meadow. Take a deep breath. Notice if the air in your meadow is warm or cold. See a plush and cozy blanket in your favorite color ahead of you. Imagine yourself walking over. Notice how comfortable the fabric feels against your hands as you touch it.

Imagine yourself lying down on the blanket and looking up at the sun streaming down toward you. Are there clouds in the sky, or is it bright blue and cloud free? What would please your senses the most? Envision it. As you lie there and look up at the sky, allow yourself to tune in to how you're feeling. Above you in the sky, spontaneously and with no effort in your vision, allow a word, color, or symbol to appear. Perhaps it comes into view for just a moment. Perhaps it stays there. Simply observe it.

As you lie there in this beautiful vision, ask yourself a question about your life like "How can I experience deeper peace and meaning?" After formulating your question, envision yourself looking at the sky and seeing what answers appear above you. Simply study it without worrying whether it's good or bad, right or wrong. Don't judge; just watch what the universe has to say to you.

- When you're ready, bring your awareness back into the room. Write about what you saw in the sky. You can reflect on what the words, colors, or symbols mean to you.

Day 64

Stress can be caused by feelings of overwhelm, something we all understand. Many issues feel beyond our control. One way to counter those feelings is through a loving-kindness meditation.

In a loving-kindness meditation, we simply direct loving, compassionate thought to those suffering, as well as those causing the suffering. By activating your compassion, you stimulate your limbic system, the part of the brain that processes emotions and empathy. This exercise can diminish self-criticism, negative thought, self-harm, and pain. By practicing loving kindness toward those who harm us, we diminish their power and control.

Begin by clearing your thoughts and repeating "May I be well. May I be happy. May I be free." After 5 minutes, turn your thoughts to others, whether you have positive or negative thoughts about them. Visualize them while repeating "May they be well. May they be happy. May they be free."

- Write a list of the events and people you focused on. Do you feel better about yourself and more aware after completing this meditation? Did you feel any negative feelings loosen and lightness enter?

Day 65

As we learned yesterday in the loving-kindness meditation, practicing compassion helps us feel more connected to life and more relaxed. Tibetan monks who are devoted to the cause of compassion (with some practicing for more than 10,000 hours) have changed the ways their brains work by radiating calm and loving acceptance toward all they encounter. Imagine such a world!

Kindness is one of the best ways to participate in this world, and a word or an action that can flip negative to positive in the blink of an eye. Now, you'll take your loving-kindness meditation on the road to others. All that is required of you today is a smile. Every smile you give is a little jolt of endorphins for you and an act of kindness toward the other person. A smile says "I don't know what is happening with you, but I wish you peace." A smile is an encouragement to keep going, we're all in this together. A smile can be a way to commiserate over a long line at the store with humor. A smile can say "You're doing great" or acknowledge a kind act from another. Put smiles into the air and see what comes back to you.

- Make a list of everyone and everything you smiled at today. How did the other person react? How did you feel?

Day 66

Today, we will invite abundance into our lives. Think of abundance as a state of having everything you want or need. The opposite of abundance is lack, the feeling like you don't have enough. It often comes from fear, the fear of not being good enough, strong enough, rich enough, or beautiful enough.

How you view your reality has a tremendous impact on the experience of your life. Let's cultivate abundance—that state of feeling safe, secure, and luxurious—and source our choices, experiences, and reality from the idea of an abundant world. I am here to affirm that you are strong and perfect exactly as you are; you have everything you need within you.

We'll do this by creating simple affirmative statements like "I am joyfully abundant," "I choose abundance in this moment," "I embody abundance with ease and effortlessness," "my life is full of friendship and laughter," or "all that I need is here." I like to write out affirmations on sticky notes and post them on the bathroom mirror or inside the medicine cabinet in the bathroom so I can see them daily.

- How do you feel about this idea of abundance? What does it evoke for you?

- Write down some more abundance affirmations, and decide where you might like to place them. Look at them as often as possible, and stay connected to all the rich abundance in your life.

Day 67

Sometimes we get caught in negative loops. Our days may feel repetitive, and our thoughts may become negative. You've learned many exercises that chase agitation and cobwebs from the mind, so today we'll focus on making changes in the way you move through the world.

Change requires awareness. It takes you out of your internal focus and requires you to engage with the world in a new way. The more new actions you take, the more your self-confidence builds. Knowing you can handle whatever pops up can build calm self-assuredness.

- Make a list of your physical habits—the way you prepare for work, the direction you take, any event that happens every day at the same time and in the same order. Now, under each entry, write how you could imagine changing the routine. Can you leave 10 minutes early and take the scenic way home from work? Could you take your lunch in a park in the sun rather than sitting in a fluorescent-lit break room? Instead of immediately reaching for that glass of white wine, what about enjoying a delicious herbal tea or fresh juice? How might you feel when you make these changes?

Day 68

Your mind is a powerful tool. Simply thinking about something calming can make you feel that way. Think back to a time when you felt a deep sense of relaxation. Maybe you were getting a deep-tissue massage or relaxing on a blanket in a sunlit park. Go deeply into that feeling of relaxation. Imagine it again. Close your eyes for a moment, and really let yourself feel it.

Now imagine a time when you felt authentic, ecstatic joy. When did you feel truly happy most recently? When was the last time that you were so immersed in the feeling of happiness that you felt for even a moment that everything else fell away? What did that experience feel like? Close your eyes for a moment, and really let yourself deepen into it.

- Write about this moment. In this journal, consider how you could re-create similar experiences.

- What was unique about each experience? What made each one stand out to you as one of authentic, deep rest, serenity, or joy?

- What was the environment like? Do you think being outdoors or indoors contributed? Was it loud or quiet?

- What type of environment brings you calmness or happiness? Which people?

Day 69

One of the top suggestions for decreasing your stress and improving your sense of peace and calm is an occasional media fast. Being bombarded with constant headlines of stressful and sometimes disturbing events is upsetting, even if we are social-ized to ignore it. Studies have shown that exposure to as little as 30 minutes of violent or disturbing imagery, from the news as well as movies, can result in up to 30 days of depressed immune function. I recommend setting aside at least one day per week in which you refrain from looking at the news and any violent media. If you try that weekly and notice that you feel a little bit less anxious, you might even consider expanding that to multi-ple days in the week.

- Try a news fast today. How did it affect your day? Did you feel like this would be a valuable exercise?

- How do you need to modify your daily routine to make this a regular practice?

Day 70

Detachment is a simple concept that can be challenging to practice. When you are detached, you observe the world without any drama from your emotions involved; you even observe yourself that way. This is why many meditation practices ask you to be nonjudgmental. It's a way to learn about yourself. When you observe without emotions, you can analyze situations more clearly and make better decisions. You become aware and in control of yourself, the only aspect of life you truly can control.

Today, I invite you to cultivate a sense of detachment. Imagine there is a quiet space around you and beyond are all of the people and events you have emotions about. They are not in your space and cannot come in. As you watch them, what do they do? Do you know how their stories turned out? Did your emotions change that outcome, or would it all happen the same way regardless of your emotions?

- Write about the attachments that you'd like to release. What are some situations in your life you can view with greater detachment? Can you step back from them starting today?

Day 71

It can be helpful to imagine taking all of your worries and anything that is preventing you from experiencing a sense of peace, putting them on a shelf, and then stepping away from them for a while. This provides space in your thoughts to recharge and de-stress. When you return later, you'll have a calmer, clearer mind.

Today, take inventory of everything that's troubling you right now with this visualization exercise. Envision yourself putting it all in a big white ball. Really pack it in there! Now, take that ball, and allow it to shrink right before your eyes. Next, place it on a shelf up and off to the side. You don't have to look at it or be aware of it in this moment. Take a deep breath, and feel yourself making room for a greater sense of peace.

After this exercise, you may find solutions for your worries rising to your conscious mind as if by magic. Others will need to be analyzed, but you can confront the worry when it rises again. Remember, worries come and go; they are just thoughts.

How did it feel to take inventory of your stressors?
Did setting them aside feel like a relief or a holiday?
Did that bring you a greater feeling of serenity?

Day 72

Today you'll set up a self-care ritual, something you do every day just for you. Set aside some time to fold this into your routine. This ritual can change; one day you might buy yourself a flower; the next day, you luxuriate in a bubble bath. More ideas for self-care include calling a beloved friend to build a sense of connection and love, sitting in the sun for 20 minutes for mood-elevating vitamin D, walking through a park at lunchtime, getting a massage, playing a game, and enjoying a laugh with a colleague or friend.

- Write down a few self-care ritual ideas.

- Next, try one! Write about your experience. Did you enjoy it? Was it relaxing? How did it feel?

Day 73

Repressed or unacknowledged emotions can greatly contribute to our stress level. Your body has an energy flow that is interrupted by repressed emotions. This could be in the form of past anger or sadness, even disappointment. If you disrupt the flow, you may disrupt the body's systems; immune function can be depressed.

Let's bring some of these emotions to light. Take a moment to ask yourself how you're feeling in this moment. For example, you might say you're feeling sleepy or anxious. Or you might say you're feeling happy, melancholy, resentful, or angry. Take some deep breaths, quiet your mind, and let yourself connect with those feelings. There's no need to judge them or push them to the surface; just let the emotions rise until you feel them. They are just something to notice and be aware of.

- What emotion came up? Can you identify it, analyze it, and begin expressing your feeling out loud?

- Can you connect the feeling to other recurring events in your life that created the same thoughts? What happened recently that created the feeling? What happened in the past? Is there a pattern?

- Do you have a safe place to speak and express your truth and then let go of it?

Day 74

In this visualization, you will connect with flow and ease by being like water. Physically, we all must have water to survive; healthy body function requires it. But there is something more about water, a mystery and energy, that makes it perfect for a visualization that sets the mind free for optimal creativity and problem-solving. Water represents a place that holds great peace and contentment as well as the unknown and the subconscious. If we allow ourselves to be like water, we can flow and put our mind and body back into balance.

Breathing deeply, imagine yourself as a current of water. You are flowing water. You are raining down from the clouds onto the earth. You are joining a river and rushing to the sea. You are flowing and moving through the ocean with sea life swimming through you. Now imagine yourself as an endless ocean. Meditate for a few minutes, imagining you are water.

- Write about your experience. What did it feel like to be water? What did you flow around? Did you flow quickly, or like a slow river? How did this motion feel?

Day 75

We've all procrastinated. There's a business call you have been dreading. It's that time of year when the gutters need cleaning You put it off from one day to the next as the stress inside builds, you know you have to do it, it's just a matter of when. Procrastination is a way we build worry into our lives. If you allow your headspace to be occupied by what you don't want to do, how will you have room to think about what you do want to do?

Silence it by using the strategy of business moguls and CEOs. Put the thing that you don't want to do at the top of your to-do list for tomorrow and *do it*. Get it done and off the list so the worry stops making noise. If you do it first thing in the morning, your day is wide open for more enjoyable tasks and adventures.

- Make a to-do list for tomorrow. What are your least favorite tasks? Move them to the top of the list, and do them first thing in the morning.

- How did it feel to complete those tasks? Was your mind freer throughout the day? Did you feel calmer overall? Write about your thoughts and feelings.

Day 76

Sometimes there are things that prevent you from experiencing your deepest sense of calm. Let's wash those away with another simple and easy visualization. Envision yourself wading into a pool of crystal-clear water. It's a natural pool surrounded by rocks. Approach a rock face, and see a beautifully cascading waterfall. This water is flowing straight down, and you can easily stand under it. Stand under that beautiful waterfall of crystal clear water. The waterfall provides the perfect water pressure—vigorous enough to clear away any stress or unwanted emotions, but gentle enough to feel good.

As you sit under your waterfall, say, "I let go of all that does not serve me." Repeat for as long as you'd like. Let the waterfall wash away negative emotion and repetitive thoughts. Concentrate on smooth, flowing water carrying it all away. Breathe deeply, in and out, throughout this exercise.

How did this visualization feel? Did you feel energized, calm, and refreshed? What emotions did you wash away as you visualized the waterfall?

Day 77

The energy that flows through our bodies does so in rivers of light. The energy that flows through our throat and neck is generally associated with self-expression. When our self-expression is not flowing, we feel tense and constricted—the opposite of expansiveness and spaciousness. Constriction leads to less inner peace and less calmness because we feel tension.

Let's do a simple exercise to open the energy in the throat so it can flow. I now invite you to tone, to emit sound. This can sound like humming or singing or even a shriek or a cry. You can use any of the following syllables as a starting point: *Ah, Oh, Eh, Ha,* or *Oo*. Or any other single-syllable sound that comes to mind, over and over. Emit these tones at varying pitches. Try different tones, and feel what feels more expansive in your throat. Take some deep breaths in between these tones, and do this with the intention of clearing the energy and helping it flow in your throat so that you can feel calmer and more expansive.

What did that feel like? Which tones did you enjoy making the most? Do you see the value of toning in this exercise?

Day 78

Reconnecting with special memories is a perfect way to lower your stress levels, taking you to a place where you felt safe, happy, and calm. Through writing, you can relive a precious memory and describe details that made it special. You'll frequently be surprised what you remember; the subconscious is like that. We are often unaware of so much that happens in the mind.

- Describe a great memory. Where did it take place? Who was there? What did it feel like? Look like? Sound like? Smell like? What was said? What wasn't said? What did you do? Would you do it again? What were your feelings about everything that happened?

- Continue building a happy-memory list. You'll be amazed how much good is in your life. Strive to create more memories that move you such as this; that's how you build a great life.

Day 79

Gratitude lists can bring peace and serenity because they offer you the chance to count your blessings and see the abundance in your life. Even on my most stressful days, I find this simple exercise to be incredibly soothing. Give it a try! You can write about the beautiful flower on your way to work, the people in your life, or the fact that you have a yoga class tomorrow. Anything goes!

- Make a list of at least 20 things for which you are grateful.

Day 80

For this meditation, find a leaf from outdoors or use a photograph. Ideally, choose a leaf that has already fallen off a tree; you'll use this leaf as a tool to foster mindfulness. Hold your leaf in your hands. Observe it. Notice its details and its texture. Immerse yourself in its color. Does it please you? Do you like it? Does it give you pleasure to look at the different textures and colors of this leaf? Bring your singular focus to the leaf as you smell it. Does it have a scent? Is it a fresh scent? Or does it lack an aroma that you can detect? Hold it in your hands. What does it feel like?

When we bring our focus to one single item, especially one from nature, it induces a greater sense of calm. Allow that to happen for you now, and enjoy the sensations that it brings.

● . What did you notice about the leaf, and how did it feel to bring your attention to it in such a focused manner? Did you have the urge to multitask or look at your phone? Reflect on your experience without judgment, and write about it.

Day 81

Set aside about 10 minutes today for a walking meditation. You can practice the meditation for longer, if you like, but you'll need at least 10 minutes to get into it. If you are inside, you can walk around your home. If you are outside or would like to go outside, you can go for a walk on a street, a path, or a trail of your choosing.

As you walk, pay attention to your feet and bring your focus to each step you take. At the same time, allow yourself to experience all the sensations around you by seeing, smelling, hearing, and feeling any sensations on your skin. Each step is like repeating a mantra in your meditation; every time your foot rises and falls your focus is drawn back to your steps and the present moment. Keep your breathing deep and steady as in any meditation. Take in all these sensations and meditative moments as you walk.

- Write about your experience with this walking meditation. What did your walk feel like? Were you barefoot? What did you notice through the soles of your feet? Was there a breeze on your skin? What did it feel like?

- What parts of your walking meditation did you enjoy, and what did you notice when you brought your attention to your feet and to your surroundings? Reflect about all of it.

Day 82

Our modern world can be anxiety-provoking. There's so much stimuli all around us—when we drive around, when we look at our phones, when we go to work, when we go on the computer, and when we watch TV. All of this stimulation can be overwhelming. Anxiety triggers cortisol in our bodies. Cortisol is produced by our adrenal glands, and it can cause an array of unhealthy physiological responses. These include high blood pressure, insulin resistance, and even high cholesterol. Taking steps to reduce cortisol and eliminate anxiety is good for your health.

Today, take conscious stock of how you feel and what evokes worry for you. By noticing what brings you worry and journaling about it, you can interrupt anxious thoughts and replace them with something positive, such as "I choose peace" or "I am here and I am safe." Any similar thought would be perfect.

- List the things that evoked worry or anxiety for you today. Did it accomplish anything for you to feel worry about these things? What are examples of positive thoughts or activities that can replace that anxiety? (Hint: Meditation is clinically proven to reduce cortisol.)

Day 83

Let's engage your imagination to help you find a deeper and more rooted sense of peace and tranquility. Imagine yourself as a wave or an emanation of light in the complete quiet of deep space. In the distance, you can see stars and a supernova. Breathe deeply. Feel the expansiveness and the openness here in deep space. Let yourself feel that level of expansion and spaciousness in your being. Let that sense of deep quiet permeate you. Let yourself be immersed in the sensations and the feelings that evoke for you.

- What came up for you during that visualization? Did it make you feel wide open and free? Or did it feel too lonely and too isolated for you? Write about it.

Day 84

Dehydration can diminish your sense of peace as one of the top causes of bodily tension and muscular discomfort. It has many causes, including hot weather, physical exertion, or things that compromise our immune system, such as a cold or flu. It's incredibly important to drink enough water and get enough electrolytes. You can infuse your water with cucumbers, celery, watermelon with mint leaves, star fruit, or strawberries with fresh basil. These all contribute electrolytes and micronutrients. You can also take potassium supplements, electrolyte drops, or homeopathic products such as bioplasma cell salts. Make sure you get enough magnesium as well; it is a crucial electrolyte, a muscle relaxant, and can improve brain function.

- In the meantime, sit with a large glass of cool water. Slowly begin to drink it in deeply. Does the water have a taste?

- Describe your body's response to the water. Did your body have an immediate reaction? Did drinking the water feel calming? Relaxing? Did any anxiety you might have been feeling diminish?

Day 85

Have you heard of the concept true north? Unlike magnetic north, the direction toward which a compass points, true north refers to the northerly direction that will take you straight to the North Pole. True north is equivalent to the most direct path arriving at your goal. True north is your life's purpose. When you know yourself, you are able to feel safe. Feelings of safety, whether physical, emotional, or mental, lead to deeper rest and calmness. Close your eyes for a minute and contemplate your true north. What is your purpose? What guides you through your day? Where does your true north lead you?

- Describe your true north, and explore what drives you, what governs your life, and what guides you. You may find deep reasons for why you do what you do.

Day 86

Forgiveness is something that we often seek after a conflict or a problem, but it can be challenging to find. It usually takes time for emotions to cool so that reconciliation is possible. People sometimes get attached to negative emotions, and forgiveness requires that you let go of it. Some people don't like to apologize or admit they are wrong. Forgiveness requires empathy for the other and a shift in your point of view. Once you forgive or are forgiven, a difficult situation can turn into a sense of calm and peaceful happiness. The connection is restored. When things feel off, we feel off. When there is something or someone to forgive, we feel it within our inner being. And, when it is righted, we feel greater peace in our hearts.

- Write down the name of a person or describe a situation where you felt you were treated unfairly or unkindly.

- Describe your emotions in as much detail as you'd like. Was the other person operating out of a place of decency, or were they in fact trying to do you harm? If you inflicted a hurt, was that your intention? Do you know why? Can you apologize or otherwise right the situation? If you were wronged, can you calmly state your position without anger and accusation?

Day 87

This simple visualization can release feelings of peace and calm wherever you are, whenever you need it. You can visualize anything anywhere, and no one knows you're doing it; it's like an invisible calming superpower you whip out when you need it.

Deep within you there is a treasure chest. It holds all the joy, peace, happiness, and serenity that you desire. Visualize a key. It's so easy to find it; it just appears in your hands with no effort. Inhale deeply, and as you exhale, bring your dominant hand up. Imagine you're holding a golden key in that hand, and bring it to any area on your body where the treasure lies. Insert it and turn the key in the lock. Breathe as you unlock this treasure chest in your body. The chest opens effortlessly. Open the lid up, and allow your treasures to circulate freely inside you. Now that you've opened and unleashed this energy, positive forces fill you. Your cortisol levels stay in balance; your energy level increases as your breath goes deeper and oxygen flows throughout your being. You've now created a space between yourself and your perceived worries.

How did it feel to open the treasure chest? Did you get a sense of what else might be inside the chest? What feelings did this exercise bring up?

Day 88

We are bombarded with so many messages about how we are not enough and how we could be better every day. Whether online, on television, or in magazines, ads for cosmetics and clothing sell us products by telling us we need to look better, thinner, more in fashion. Ads for cleaning products and household items convince us that we need to try harder to make our homes perfect. But guess what? These messages are lies. Without that spotless kitchen island, you're still a great cook. Even in your old jeans, you're perfect exactly as you are. You don't need different makeup, new clothes, or a robot vacuum to be your best. Accepting yourself is a crucial component of feeling a true sense of peace.

Contemplate this statement, repeating it in your head or aloud: "I accept myself on all levels exactly as I am. I accept myself deeply and with great love."

- Write about your experience. How did it feel to say these affirmations? Was it challenging? What are other ways that you can practice self-acceptance?

Day 89

When your heart feels full of goodness, you experience more peace and calm in your life. Today, we will re-attach to the power of the human heart as it drives energy throughout you whenever it beats. Think of it as an engine within you, pumping out good intention, light, and love to the world. Now that's a powerful idea.

Bring your dominant hand up to the pulse point on the side of your neck and find a spot where you can feel your pulse under your fingertips. Tune in to that pulse. Feel it beating within you. Let your pulse be your singular focus. Breathe deeply as you focus on the beat of your heart and move into a meditative state. Sit with that sensation for a few minutes. Notice how it feels.

Describe what it felt like to focus on your own heartbeat. Did it bring you deeper within yourself? As you followed your deep breathing in and out, was there a change in what you felt on your neck? When you connected with the power of your own heart, did you feel grounded and calm? Write down all your thoughts and sensations.

Day 90

Building upon the previous exercises that have grounded us through self-knowledge, self-acceptance, and self-love, take 10 or 20 minutes to contemplate what you like about yourself. Only when you like and accept yourself can you feel a deep sense of peace and contentment. You can recall an event, such as remembering the time you stepped in and defended someone. Or you can explore a quality you possess. For instance, you could be a fine listener or a comedian. Both are important to our experiences. Part of your strengths might be physical; for example, your strong arms have lifted heavy groceries.

In these qualities, you'll begin to see what is unique about you; the unique set of characteristics and qualities that make you so you. You may see patterns of strength emerge, such as "I really can keep a secret" or "I do not let friends down." Focus on your good qualities only.

- Write down your list. Does it create a picture of a person you are proud to be? Can you operate more from your strengths, focusing on helping yourself and those around you?

Day 91

Take a moment to consider the idea of bliss, the state of utter happiness and contentment. Have you felt it? I have, lying in the warm fall sun in my backyard. A friend encountered bliss as she floated on her back in the ocean. Bliss is not about the high of achievement; it's the joyous simplicity of feeling free, happy, and alive. You knew it as a child, and it's time to get reacquainted.

- Ask yourself these questions: Have you felt bliss? How did it feel? Where were you, and what were you doing? Can you imagine a place right now where you might find bliss? Can you go there? Write your responses in this journal.

Day 92

One important aspect of calmness and serenity is having faith in the benevolence of the world. Believing the world will catch you when you fall can be a challenge at times. But every life is filled with bounty and goodness; you just need to observe and acknowledge it.

We love stories about a struggling person who sleeps in their car before suddenly, as if by magic, the world turns them into a movie star. You may have your own stories of struggle right before landing an opportunity that turns it all around. Some days, the goodness of world is much less dramatic. For example, you have tea with a friend and they connect you with your next career option.

- Write a list of the moments when you encountered the loving kindness of the world. What happened? How did you feel? Are there more events and people who have blessed you than you first thought? Do you feel the goodness in your life?

Day 93

Healers in the ancient Far East learned that the bottoms of our feet correspond to neural pathways that release tension and stress in the body. By simply massaging different areas on the soles of your feet, you can greatly diminish stress levels, clear toxins from your system, and fall asleep.

These ancient healers, through trial and error, learned the sole of the big toe is a gatekeeper for the backed-up energy in the body that manifests as stress. To release it and sleep, you will now take one page out of the ancient healing art known as "reflexology" and rub the soles of your own feet.

Find a comfortable position where you can easily reach the bottoms of both big toes. You can work each toe with both hands or work both toes simultaneously. The goal is to massage and roll the bottoms of your big toes vigorously for 10 minutes, releasing any built-up energy through your nervous system. Agitation should give way to a refreshing calm as your body relaxes into a new state of being. Sleep should come much easier now.

- Write about how you felt before, during, and after your foot massage. Do you feel more relaxed? Were you ready to sleep?

Day 94

Get comfortable and take a few deep breaths to prepare for another visualization exercise. This visualization may inspire you to change things in your life or encourage you to keep them the same. Any of these outcomes is perfect. Remember, this isn't a goal-oriented exercise. It's intended to foster greater levels of self-awareness. You'll also feel a sense of calm immersed in a bath of green, contemplating the arc of your life. As your awareness increases, any feelings of powerlessness decrease because you are reminded that you have choices; you just have to see them and make a move, as needed.

Imagine yourself walking down a path or dirt road through a forest. A green line of light appears on your path. Understand that you are walking the life path that you have created for yourself. See this symbolic green line stretching out in front of you on the forest floor. Does it feel good to you, or would you like to change it? Allow yourself to feel the answer. If you are content with your path as it is now, then just keep moving along. You can choose a new path any time.

- What was the experience of walking your invisible path through the forest like? How did you feel when you discovered a pathway that innately felt like the one that's right for you?

Day 95

This simple breathing exercise is perfect to rid yourself of any bad thoughts or feelings that stand between you and calm. It can be used to clean out illness and dark thoughts; you can literally blow the anger out of your body, freeing you to deal calmly with whatever is causing the feeling. Blowing out useless emotion and negative energy makes room for the good stuff to flow in.

Sit or lie where you feel comfortable. You should have lots of fresh air for this exercise. Pull a deep breath into your belly, and imagine the situation that has caused you unpleasant feelings. Hold the breath for three beats. Now, exhale the feeling out in a long forceful emptying of your lungs. Repeat. Continue working on an issue until you feel its power leave.

- Make a list of the issues that you worked on with your breath. How did you feel before you started breathing? How did you feel afterward? Did any thoughts come to you that changed your perceptions of your worries? Do you feel a sense of calm when you exhale density?

Day 96

Meditation creates a space in the mind from which you can make decisions in a calm rational manner; these two activities turn off the noise in your head. In yoga, stretching joins meditation to calm the noise in your body, the place where unresolved, unprocessed emotion eventually goes to live.

Simple stretching unknots the body, releases endorphins, and promotes blood flow. It's great to help you fall asleep as well. You decrease your potential for injury because stretching keeps your muscles limber and flexible. A short stretch reenergizes body and mind.

Stand with your legs shoulder width apart. Raise your arms to your sides slowly, then raise them over your head, bringing your palms together. Gently move your raised palms backward, creating a small gentle arch in your spine. You may feel a tingling at the base of your back. Now, slowly fold yourself at the waist, spilling your arms forward toward your feet. If you can't reach them, that's perfectly okay! The point is to stretch in a way that relaxes but doesn't hurt your body. Repeat your stretches for 5 to 10 minutes.

- How did your mind and body feel at the beginning? How did you feel afterward?

- Can you think of more stretches to add to your practice?

Day 97

Creativity is one of the most calming activities in life; you lose a sense of space and time as you magically live inside a vision, bringing it into existence for yourself and others. The outside world falls away as you focus on your abilities to make something good and beautiful.

People get strange ideas about creativity. "Oh, I couldn't possibly draw. I have no talent!" I say, "Says who?" We all know everything is in the eye of the beholder, and it's not the finished product you should obsess over here but the doing.

Today's activity is simple. You'll either make something, or plan to make something, and then do it. Choreograph a dance or take a pottery class. Buy a picture frame, and decorate it for a friend. String lights across your bedroom, and imagine they are stars. Get inspiration from the endless images online and in magazines.

- What did you make? How did you feel as you were creating? Did the cares of the world drop away as you lived with the joy of your imagination?

- Can you see yourself doing other fun projects? List of all of them, and come back to them. Make creativity a part of your life.

Day 98

Imagine yourself in a forest and rising above the woods toward bright blue sky; in that pure space you can envision how you'd love your life to be. As you imagine lifting above the trees, feel as if you are elevating above your concerns and worries.

Surrounded by the calming blue sky, I want you to ask yourself some questions. In this perfect place without limits, what would a sense of calmness and serenity look like in your life? How would it feel? Next, ask yourself without judgment if there is anything blocking you from experiencing that calmness in your day-to-day life. It could be you. It could be a situation. It could be a person or persons. It could be your schedule.

Lastly, ask yourself about a potential solution for those things that get in your way. What can help you overcome these obstacles with ease and grace?

- Write down your answers to these questions. Refrain from judging your thoughts, and simply sit with your answers in a quiet location for a few minutes.

Day 99

You are connected to Mother Earth deeply. She provides us with air, water, sunlight, and food. Animals and plants all around us are deeply linked to our beings. We are all part of Earth. We're all interconnected.

Today, you are to draw on everything you've ever felt and ever seen to make a list of the Earth's goodness. How does sand feel on the soles of your feet? How sweet is freshly picked corn? Can you describe the cool stream you played in as a child? Do you smell fall leaves and see the faces of your parents raking in the yard? How does the fur of an animal feel in your hands? Can you remember when you first saw the ocean, or was it always in your life, a huge force that was just there? How did you feel looking at it? Did it have a smell, a sound?

Keep your list at hand, and add to it as often as possible. Do you see a list of wonder and miracles forming? Can you deepen your love and gratitude for the Earth through all that you do?

Day 100

You've arrived at the last day of your journey toward calm. Now it's time to reflect on your new skills and get them working in your day-to-day life.

- As you go back over this journal and what you wrote, what did you discover about yourself that surprised you the most? What did you observe about yourself?

- Can you calmly and clearly see any patterns in your life? Can you imagine adjusting the ones that cause you discomfort? Do you feel more in touch with where stress lives in your body?

- List your favorite exercises, and describe how you can integrate them into your life long term. What activities would you like to practice more often? Which have been the most effective?

What a journey this has been. I'm proud of you. You've done wonderfully.

About the Author

Amy Leigh Mercree is a best-selling author, holistic health expert, and medical intuitive. Mercree speaks and teaches internationally, sharing Next Level Healing, Meet Your Guides, Mindfulness Meditation, and Bestseller Bootcamp classes.

Mercree is the author of 14 books, including *A Little Bit of Mindfulness*, *The Mood Book*, *A Little Bit of Goddess*, and three "Little Bit of" journals.

Mercree has been featured in *Glamour* magazine, *Women's Health, Inc.* magazine, *Shape*, *The Huffington Post*, *YourTango*, *Soul and Spirit* magazine, *mindbodygreen*, CBS, NBC, FOX, Hello Giggles, *Reader's Digest*, *O, The Oprah Magazine*, *Forbes*, *First for Women*, *Country Living*, *Bustle*, *Elite Daily*, *Thrive Global*, *Poosh*, *Well+Good*, and many more. She is fast becoming one of the most quoted women on the web. See what all the buzz is about @AmyLeighMercree on social media.

To download your free Deep Calmness Toolkit and find your peace and calm right now, go to www.amyleighmercree.com /deepcalmnesstoolkit (password: CALM).

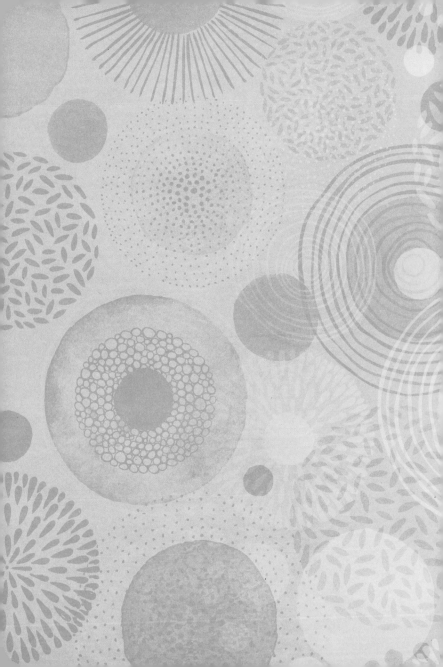